PENPALS *for* Handwriting

Year 3 Practice Book (7–8 years)

By **Gill Budgell & Kate Ruttle**

Supported by the
National Handwriting Association
Promoting good practice

Contents

CAMBRIDGE UNIVERSITY PRESS

Practise the joins.

 *mus ic ian sev en*

Write the words.

 *musician seven crane*

Write the sentence.

 *We can see seven musicians in a row on a crane.*

Practise the pattern.

Read and write the words.

c ov er

cover

mem or ise

memorise

s ci ence

science

Practise the joins.

 ll   ll   ll   tt   tt   tt

Write the words.

 Hello little balloon

Write the joke.

 What did the little balloon
say to the pin?

"Hello Buster!"

Practise the pattern.

Read and write the words.

c all ed

called

p add led

paddled

ti ck led

tickled

Practise the joins.

 sh   sl   st   sk

Read and write the words.

Write the words.

 ship   slip   sting   skin

should

Make compound words by joining words from each box.

ship	chop	brush	fish
paint	skate	wreck	shake
milk	star	stick	board

star

finish

skeleton

friendship

Practise the pattern.

Practise the joins.

sw si se sm sn sp su

Write the words.

submarine   secret   submit

Write the report.

Sensational news story
Yesterday, a secret supersonic
submarine submerged in the
Irish Sea. Is it on a spying
mission?

Read and write
the words.

surprise

smiles

snorkel

sister

university

Practise the pattern.

ſ ſ ſ ſ ſ ſ ſ ſ

Practise the joins.

 *sa   sc   sd   sg   so   sq*

Write the words.

 *sensational   disguises   squash*

Write the poster.

Disguises for sale:

scary squirrel
wise scientist
sad stegosaurus
awesome spaceman

Read and write the words.

wisdom

square

biscuit

Wednesday

safari

Practise the pattern.

Practise the joins.

 rb   rh   rk   rl   rt

Write the words.

 *sparkling   whirling   flirting*

Write the poem.

Sparkling, the leaves
Whirl and twirl
Curl and swirl
Flirting in the wind

Practise the pattern.

Read and write the words.

dart

spark

rhythm

early

harbour

Practise the joins.

ri   ru   rn   rp

Write the words.

surprise   descriptions

Write the poster.

the rising sun
a burning carpet
a charity run
an April shower

Describe these pictures for a friend to draw.

Practise the pattern.

Read and write the words.

rice

turnip

runner

chorus

purpose

Practise the joins.

 _ra   rd   rg   ro_

Write the words.

 _orange   emergency   survival_

Write the question.

 _In an emergency, would you_
make a cardboard raft?

Oh rats!
I'm drowning!

Practise the pattern.

Read and write the words.

board

round

afraid

circle

argument

9

Practise the joins.

 *are   ere   ure   ore   ire*

Write the words.

 *feature   adventures*

Write the poster.

> ## Treasure Island
> ## Pirates Galore
>
> Showing here for one week only.
>
> Pre-book directly online
> or here at The Spire Theatre.

Read and write the words.

core
measure
parents
increase
remember

Practise the pattern.

 *eee eee eee*

Practise the letters.

 g j y f b p q x z

Write the words.

 crazy   pen   breaks

Write the rules.

Break letters

We do not join from break letters.
Most break letters end with a
pencil stroke to the left;
x and z never join.

Practise the pattern.

Read and write the words.

bigger

breakfast

jogger

mystery

injured

11

Practise the joins.

if   ef   af   of

Write the words.

aircraft   safe   refuel

Read and write the words.

often

Write the letter. Put the parts in order.

This afternoon I took the book to the local airfield.

Dear Grandfather

Thank you for the book on aircraft. I'm very grateful for it.

Hopefully, we will see you soon. Lots of love Alfie

prefer

proof

terrified

spacecraft

Practise the pattern.

Practise the joins.

 *fl   fl   fl   ft   ft   ft*

Write the words.

 *flash   flood   inflatables*

Write the sentences.

Terrible flash floods have affected families living here. Elderly people were airlifted from rooftops this afternoon. Others are still afloat on rafts and inflatable dingies.

Practise the pattern.

Read and write the words.

flag

lift

flavour

soften

camouflage

13

Practise the joins.

fe　　fi　　fu　　fr　　fy

Read and write the words.

Write the words.

five　　funny　　friends

film

Write the sentences. Fill the gaps with your friends' names.

My friends are wonderful.

_____ *is funny.*

_____ *is confident.*

_____ *is fearless.*

_____ *is friendly.*

frill

life

satisfy

certificate

Practise the pattern.

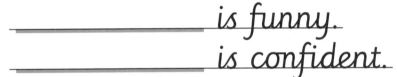

Practise the joins.

 *fo   fo   fa   fa*

Write the words.

 *four facts for you to fathom*

Write the sentences. Write *fact* **or** *fiction* **after each.**

 The first fossil was found last Friday.

A firefighter wears a uniform.

A fox leaves no footprints

Practise the pattern.

Read and write the words.

forwards

farm

surface

before

information

Practise the joins.

 *ff ff ff ff*

Write the words.

 *toffee   waffle   coffee*

Write the dialogue.

 *"Can I offer you a toffee or a waffle?" Effie asked Asiff. "Both affect me badly and I'd be sniffling and snuffling."*

Practise the pattern.

Read and write the words.

offer

afford

traffic

difficult

scaffolding

Practise the joins.

 rr   rr   rr   rr

Write the words.

 hurry   carry   flurry

Write the address.

Harriet Carrington
The Old Barracks
7 Barracuda Parade
Quarry Hill Estate
Torrenton Barretteshire
SM7 8RR

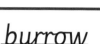
Read and write the words.

burrow

carry

horrible

quarrel

gooseberries

Practise the pattern.

Practise the joins.

 ss   ss   ss   ss

Write the words.

 criss-cross   loss   hiss

Write the sentence.

 The harmless snake hissed
breathlessly as it
criss-crossed over
the mossy wilderness.

Practise the pattern.

Read and write
the words.

unless

cross

address

princess

impossible

Practise the joins.

 *qu qu qu qu*

Write the words.

 *quiz   question   quick*

Write the quiz. Answer the questions.

 1. Must all the faces of a cube be equal-sized squares?

2. Can a square be a quarter of a quadrilateral?

3. Continue this sequence: 3, 6, 9 ...

Practise the pattern.

 Read and write the words.

quack

quite

quiet

liquid

earthquake

Practise the joins.

ly ily ally ly ily ally

Write the words.

merrily   hilly   diagonally

Write the words. Keep your down strokes parallel.

lightly   gloomily   kindly

cheerfully   wonderfully   funnily

Write each in a sentence.

Practise the pattern.

Read and write
the words.

cheerfully

completely

equally

happily

difficulty

Write the rhyme.

Patiently, the fisherman waits.
Will he catch...
A mattress spring or welly boot?
A croquet mallet, a wooden flute?
A pirate's earring, a buffalo's fleece?
Or just a moment
for quiet and peace?

Read and write
the words.

asked

demanded

requested

wished

commanded

Practise the pattern.

Write the heading.

Dialogue jokes

Write the joke. Check your letters are evenly spaced.
Check your apostrophe has a letter space.

Read and write
the words.

"Doctor, doctor, I think I'm a dog!" cried the patient.

"Sit on the couch and we'll talk about it," soothed the doctor.

"But I'm not allowed on the couch!" barked the patient.

they're

we'll

we're

it's

should've

Practise the pattern.

Write the heading.

Where are the Poles?

Write the text. Allow space for one or two letter os between each word.

The North Pole is the point on
Earth that is the furthest north.
It is found in the middle of the
Arctic Ocean. The South Pole
is furthest south. It is near the
centre of the continent
called Antarctica.

Read and write
the words.

heading

sub-heading

paragraph

sentence

clause

Practise the pattern.

Write the heading.

Are your LETTERS .... cap height

the same size? .... Lower case x height letters

Draw the table. Write the words in the table.

Word class	Punctuation mark	Type of sentence

command   *adverb*
apostrophe *comma*
noun   *adjective*

Practise the pattern.

⌒⌒⌒   ⋃⋃⋃   ⌒⌒⌒   ⋃⋃⋃   ⌒⌒⌒

Read and write the words.

vowel

consonant

alphabet

letter

twenty-six

Write the heading.

Fire ·········· Check that your writing
is round and flowing

Write the poem.

"Fire! Fire!" says Obadiah.
"Where? Where?" says Mrs. Pear.
"Behind the rocks," says Dr. Fox.
"Put it out!" says Mr. Trout.
"I've no bucket,"
says Lord MacTucket.
"Use my shoe,"
says You Know Who.

Practise the pattern.

Read and write
the words.

poem

rhyme

rhythm

verse

title

25

Write the heading.

Keep your downstrokes parallel and the ascenders the same height.

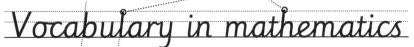

Vocabulary in mathematics

Draw the table. Sort and write the words into two lists.

Words about shapes	Words about numbers

horizontal   _circle_   _estimate_
addition   _thousand_   _subtraction_
cuboid   _vertical_

Practise the pattern.

Read and write the words.

breathe

address

brilliant

schedule

mathematical

Write the heading.

How many letters?

Keep descenders
the same length.   Keep your downstrokes parallel.

Write the words in order of the number of letters.

beautifully   mystery   knowledge

importantly   although

thoughtful   opposite   impossibility

belief   often   experiment

Practise the pattern.

Read and write
the words.

February

bicycle

eighth

difficulty

camouflaged

Practise the joins.

 rs   rs   rs   rs

Write the words.

 his   hers   theirs   ours

Write the sentences.

It's hers.

No, it's not yours.

Yes, it's ours.

No, it's theirs.

Read and write the words.

yours

sisters

brothers

theirs

Mrs.

Practise the pattern.

Write the heading.

Break letters.

Write the break letter rules.

We join to but not from g, j, y, b, p.
We do not join to or from x and z.

Write the text and check your break letters.

The Wright Brothers
Wilbur and Orville Wright liked
engineering challenges. They owned a
bicycle repair shop. Later, they made a
glider. They put an engine in their glider
and invented the world's first aeroplane.

Practise the pattern.

Read and write the words.

enjoying

brother

above

giggle

alphabet

Write the heading.

Fast and fluent

Write the words.

musician   _balloon_   _friendship_

stegosaurus   _rhythm_   _adventure_

Write the sentence very neatly.

The quick brown fox
jumped over the lazy dog.

Now write the sentence as fast as you can. What happens to your writing when you write very fast?

Review your writing using this checklist.

1. Are there any joins you need to practise?

2. Are your letters the right size (capitals too)?

3. Is the spacing between letters and words good?

4. Are your ascenders and descenders parallel?

5. Did your hand move smoothly over the page as you wrote?

Write the alphabet in capital letters.

A B C D E F G H I J K L M N
O P Q R S T U V W X Y Z

Write the book titles.

'My Criminal Life'
by Robin Banks

'The Ghost Hunters'
by Terry Fied

'Falling Trees'
by Tim Burr

Practise the pattern.

Read and write the words.

book

title

author

page

chapter